# THE INVISIBLE VILLAIN

**Ian McMillan** is a poet, writer, performer and broadcaster. He is poet-in-residence at Barnsley Football Club, Yorkshire TV's investigative poet and a regular on BBC Radio 4's *Poetry Please*, *Booked* and *Front Row*. He has written many books of poetry, including *It's Just Like Watching Brazil*, which recounts Barnsley FC's breathtaking season in the premiership. Find out more about Ian at www.ian-mcmillan.co.uk

**Alan Rowe** has been working as an illustrator for 16 years since he graduated from Kingston University. He lives in Sutton, Surrey with his partner, who is also an illustrator, three children, two cats, two goldfish and a room full of toy robots.

Also available from Macmillan Children's Books

The Very Best of Ian McMillan

I Did Not Eat the Goldfish
Poems by Roger Stevens

The Colour of My Dreams
Poems by Peter Dixon

# THE INVISIBLE VILLAIN

poems by
## Ian McMillan

illustrated by
## Alan Rowe

00470

**Macmillan Children's Books**

First published 2002
by Macmillan Children's Books
a division of Macmillan Publishers Ltd
20 New Wharf Road, London N1 9RR
Basingstoke and Oxford
www.panmacmillan.com

Associated companies throughout the world

ISBN 0 330 39845 8

Text copyright © Ian McMillan 2002
Illustrations copyright © Alan Rowe 2002

3 5 7 9 8 6 4

A CIP catalogue record for this book is available from the British Library.

Printed by Mackays of Chatham plc, Chatham, Kent.

# Contents

# The Invisible Villain Who Doesn't Do Anything

He's been. Again.
In this room,
In this very room.
The Invisible Villain Who Doesn't Do Anything.

The chairs. The table.
Just as they were.
The cat, just there,
asleep by the fire.

The mother. The dad.
The knitting. The telly.
He's been, I tell you.
Yes, I can smell him.

He's been. Again.
In this room.
In this very room.
The Invisible Villain Who Doesn't Do Anything.

# Leaf, Root, Branch

Note: leaf, root, branch is an old English form in which a poem about a forest has to contain the word leaf or root or branch in each line and has to contain the same number of lines as there are letters in leaf, root or branch, and has to end in the word Forest. Sounds complex: it ain't! Here are some examples from 'McMillan's Forest Boke' of 973AD.

## Leaf

I blend in like a leaf,
leaf green as my shirt,
a fat leaf in tights,
fat leaf hiding in a forest.

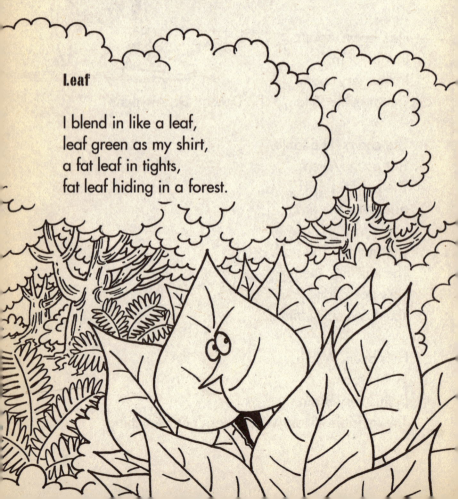

## Root

I chew at you, root
root stronger than teeth
root shatters my teeth
fling root in the forest.

## Branch

I rub twig on branch,
fire will come from branch.
branch rubbing for days,
branch will not make smoke,
branch rubbing for weeks
branch worst in the forest!

# Queue

QUEUE

|||||||||||||||||||||||||||||||||||||||||||||||||||||||||||||||||

VALENTINE'S DAY QUEUE

||||||X|||||||||||||X|||||||||||||X|||||||||||||||||||X|||||||||||

QUEUE FOR A SCARY RIDE

||||||||||||||OOOOOOOO||||||||||||||||OOOOOOO||||||||||AAAA

QUEUE WITH DOGS

|||||||||||FRFRF||||||RF||||||||||RFRF|||||||||||||||RFRFRF|||||||FII

QUEUING FOR DAYS

IZIZIZIZIZIZIZIZIZIZIZIZIZIZIZIZIZIZIZIZIZIZIZIZIZIZIZ

# Robinson Crusoe's Wise Sayings

You can never have too many turtle's eggs.
I'm the most interesting person in this room.
A beard is as long as I want it to be.

The swimmer on his own doesn't need trunks.
A tree is a good clock.
If you talk to a stone long enough you'll fall asleep.

I know it's Christmas because I cry.
Waving at ships is useless.
Footprints make me happy, unless they're my own.

# The Destiny Girls

Mum just stood there
At the car boot sale.
Her eyes were watering.
And she was looking upwards

At a vapour trail
Chalking the blue sky.
Dad was holding a flower pot,
One of fifteen,
All different sizes,
For two pounds.

He walked over to Mum,
Clutching the flowerpot;
She held something up to him,
It was an old-fashioned vinyl single.

I walked over to have a look:
It was called 'He Loves Me'
By The Destiny Girls.

Mum was crying.
Still looking up at the vapour trail
Chalking the blue sky,
And I wanted to ask what was happening.

Dad said to me
'She had a beautiful voice, your grandma,
could have been a star. This was her single,
her band, The Destiny Girls, got to about number 32 . . .'

Dad had never talked about Grandma before.
Mum hadn't either.

She didn't speak now,
Just looked up at the vapour trails
Chalking the blue sky.

'They could have been famous,'
said Dad,
'If they hadn't got on that plane . . .'

Mum said,
'At least somebody bought it,
even though it's ended up here,
I'll buy it now, put it with the others.'

'He Loves Me'
By The Destiny Girls.

Overhead the planes hummed.

# The Cage, Clipstone Colliery, Nottinghamshire

The sky holds its greyness,
Is about to spill it
Like someone about to spill dirty water from a bowl;
It's going to rain

But over in the corner
Of the sky's handkerchief
The sun is burning a misty hole in the clouds;
It'll be sunny later.

As the men gather in their helmets
At the cage's door
They are thinking about the sky;
Not the greyness, but the hole in the
    mist;
It's time to go down.

You can't think about rain
When you're going underground
Just think about the sun,
Just think about the sun

Waiting for you, tomorrow.

# Just a Minute

(written on the morning of 3/2/01)

This morning I woke up early,
Glanced at the clock:
Four minutes past five
On a cold morning in February.

February the third to be exact,
2001. All dates only come once
And then they go,
Over the day's hill, waving goodbye.

All times never stay long;
'Soon' becomes 'afterwards',
'Now' becomes 'then'. But this moment
Was more precious than most:

05 04 03 02 01,
Here for just a minute then gone.


PS:
I can't wait for the first light
On the fourth of March next year,
06 05 04 03 02,
Can you?

# Lights Action

I sneak out at night,
Alter traffic lights.

In the dark
I creep to crossroads
With my tin of paint.

I make the red blue,
And the road becomes the sea.

The orange I paint silver,
Turning the streets precious and cold,

And I cover the green with purple,
And the town looks like it lives
Inside a plum's skin.

Blue, orange, purple.
Purple, blue, orange.
Orange, purple, blue.

I sit and watch them change
Until Dawn's glow
Sends me home.

# Lovely Counting Rhyme

One, two
Buckle my sock.

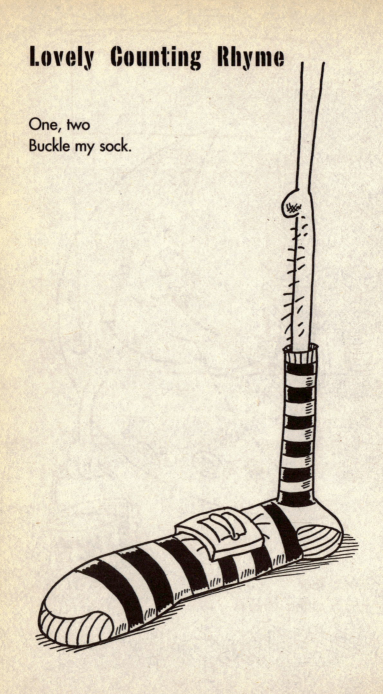

Three, four
Knock at the window.

Five, six
Pick up trees,

Seven, eight
Lay them bent.

Nine, ten
A big fat turkey.

# Name Poeb

When I get fed up,
I just change the letters in my name.
Boring old Ian McMillan becomes

Dan McMillan: detective in a hat.
Iaz McMillab: being from the planet Skarx

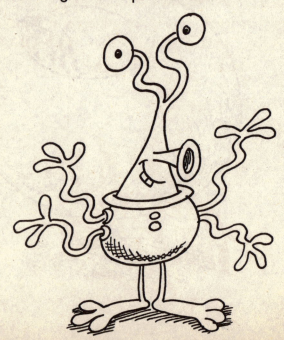

Isn McMxllbd: the spy whose name is a code.
Don MoMolloo: I'm a big fat opera singer.

In Mln: text message kid.
Iaa MaMaaaaa: mummy's boy.
Izz MzMzzzzz: asleep for a thousand years.
Ron M.C. Miller: butcher with a shop on the high
     street.

Iron McMillion: I wear lots of jewels

Hen McMilkbottle: winner of gold at the Silly Name
    Olympics

Aeon McMillan: oldest man in the world.

Ill MIMIlll: am I a name or a number?

Ian McMeal on: I like my food.

Ina McMillan: I'm a girl.

I Mill: I'd better see a doctor.

Dean McMillan: detective in a hat.

# Moon and Stars

The stars are scattered like salt
from the Moon's fish and chips

then the clouds blot them out
like the Moon's licked its lips.

# Last Friday Near the Shed

I was digging and I found a box.
I opened it and found
an old red cape
a torn red mask
some mouldy red underpants
and a gun that shot red sauce.
So it was true.
My Grandad really was
THE TOMATO.

All those years when he told us stories
about holding up the bus
and making all the passengers get off
just so that he could spray them with red sauce
he was telling the truth.

Imagine that.
My Grandad: THE TOMATO.

So I wonder if my Grandma
really was
SQUID GIRL?

I'll get my spade.

# Cat Walking Across the Grass

It's
     a

ginger

sun in
     a

green
     sky

ears pushed

back

     head

held

     high

# THE MOON IS AN EGG

1. Half-moon

Boiled,
In the night's cup

## 2. Frosty night

The yolk
And the white
Surrounding


## 3. Moonlight through Clouds

The scrambled egg
Scattered on my plate


## 4. Moon reflected in a Lake

The bald man
Eating a boiled egg


## 5. New Moon

I found this tiny piece of shell
On the dark blue carpet

# Ten One-Line Poems About Sport

**Golf**
That white moon in the blue sky, orbiting.

**Cricket**
Long late-afternoon shadows as the bowler runs.

**Basketball**
The clock runs down slower than the players.

**Swimming**
Moment of stillness before the start: water-mirror.

**Snooker**
The giant's necklace broke and the beads fell on to
     the grass.

## Football
This net's for catching slippery goalfish!

## Marathon
Last metre: the best and the worst.

## Rugby
Flying Easter egg under the H

## High Jump
The air holds me like a hand, then lets me go.

## Cycling
Here come the fastest paper boys and girls in the
world!

# HERE COMES THE ANTS! LOOK OUT, THEY'RE ATTACKING THE PICNIC!

""""""""""""""""""""

"""""""""""" """ ' ' ' ' ' ' ' ' ' ' ' ' ' ' ' ' ' ' ' ' ' ' ' ' ' ' "

'
'
'
'
'
'
'
'

""""""""""""""""""""""""""""""    A
                                  AA
                                  AAA

# Hats of my Grandma

Red:
Bad mood granny
Roaring like a lion.

Green:
Laughing lady,
Young as her smile.

Blue:
Poorly gran,
Sniffing like a dripping tap.

Yellow:
Forgetful woman:
That's her sister's hat!

# Trees Sleep Standing Up

Trees sleep standing up,

And as dawn comes

You can hear them snoring

In the leaf-tickling breeze.

# Grandad McMillan

I only have one memory
Of my dad's dad,
Grandad McMillan

He's holding up
A hot-water bottle.
It's a red one.

'Who sat on this
And burst it?'
He is saying.

He's cross
His big moustache
Is moving

As he speaks
The hot-water bottle
Is dripping.

I'm crying
My brother is watching TV.
My mother is knitting.

That's my Grandad McMillan.

He's a photo album

With one photo in it.

Just one,

Fading.

# Story Time

Sorry Dad, but
As soon as you start
Telling your stories
I really want to go to sleep.

I'm sure
They're really interesting stories
About how you nearly . . .
Sorry Dad, nodded off there a minute.

Right, I'm awake now.
Tell me about how you nearly
Played for England.
Gosh, I'm tired.

I think I'll go to bed soon.
Sorry Dad, but
Were you saying something?
One of your interesting stories?

# Cutting My Fingernails

Piles of new moons
In the sink

Fragments of me
Down the plughole

Little smiles
In the tap's waterfall

# All Shook Up

Grandad's got a bottle of Elvis sweat,
He keeps it in a jar in his wardrobe

He showed it to me once, one Summer Sunday;
Just a few drops, glinting in the sun.

'He turned and flicked his hair,' Grandad said,
'one night in Las Vegas, and I happened

to have the jar with me.' Grandad stood up,
holding the jar up like Elvis

might hold a microphone.
'Grandma says it's water from the tap,'

he said, 'but don't you believe her.
This is Elvis sweat. Real Elvis sweat.'

# A Very Funny Poem

This hahahahahaha! Sorry.
This po hahahahaha!
Is so hahahahahaha!
Funny

That hahahahahaha! Sorry.
That I hahahahaha!
Can hardly hahahahahahahahahaha!
Write it down.

Sorry.

This hahahahahahahahahahahahahaha!
This chicken hahahahahahahahahaha!
Was hahahahaha! playing hahahaha!
The piano hahahahahahahahahahahahahaha

Hahahahahahaha! Sorry. Hahahahahaha!
Hahahahaha!
Hahahaha!
Haha!
Ha!

Sorry.

# Postman Pat's Brothers

(It helps if you try and sing these to the Postman Pat tune)

Milkman Jim
Milkman Jim
His favourite milk
is semi skim-

med

Postman Pete
Postman Pete
Gave up his job
'cos he had bad feet

can't do any walking
just does lots of talking

In the Home for Retired Postmen
down our street.


Binman Bill
Binman Bill
Got flattened by a runaway bin lorry that careered
out of control down a very steep hill.

Baths attendant Ron
Baths attendant Ron
With his black and white striped trunks
on
Early in the morning
He puts in the chlorine . . .
till all the nasty nasty germs have gone.

# Change

This pound coin
Spent years down a drain
Washed there by freezing winter rain.

This pound coin
Ended up on a beach
Just beyond a baby's reach.

This pound coin
Was found by a lad
Who hid it from his mum and dad.

This pound coin
Lived in his pocket
Till he'd saved up enough to buy a rocket.

This pound coin
Was spent in a shop
On a rocket to make your eyes go pop.

This pound coin
Flew up in the sky
Waving the distant ground bye-bye.

This pound coin
Fell down again
Through the freezing winter rain

This pound coin
Ended up in the drain
And then the whole story begins again.

# As He Prepared to Go to a Concert

Uncle Tony's flapping flares
Caught the wind from the open door;
He was taken unawares
And rose three feet from the kitchen floor.

Uncle Tony shouted 'Help!'
As his flares were lifted by a gust
That sent him skywards with a yelp
And a cloud of swirling dandruff dust.

Now higher than the evening star
In the heavens Tony flies;
If you can't see where his trousers are
Just listen for his distant cries.

Somewhere beyond the big full moon
Uncle Tony flies through space:
He'll be passing over your house soon,
A happy smile on his hippy face.

# Lost Things

## 1. Tape

A bowl of chucked spaghetti.
The web of a plastic spider.
This net has caught a tree.

Who played this music,
Then threw it away?
Who wound the car window down
And flung the tape
As far as it will go?

And who will play it again,
Rewind it, mend it,
Hear the scratched songs in a room?

A tangle of brown roads.
Wool from a shiny sheep.
A snake too long for the world.

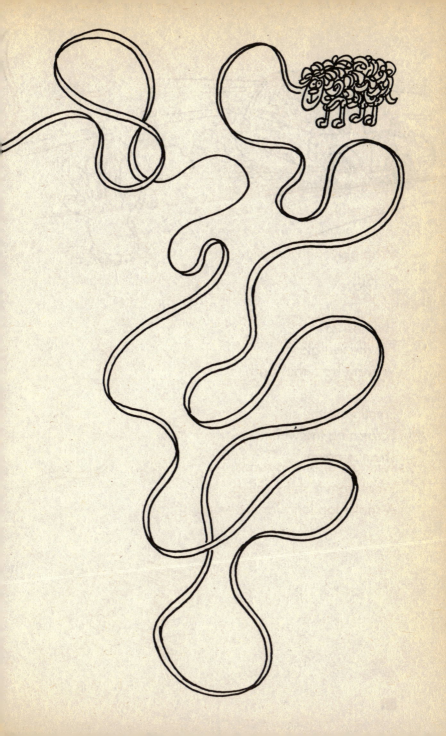

## 2. Glove

Thumbs up
For the lost glove
Waving from the road,

Pointing to the sky,
Scratching the white line,
Thumbs down.

# Some Sayings That Never Caught On

He's as daft as a pineapple!
Time is just like custard!
She swims like a cactus!

He's as daft as a cactus!
Time is just like a pineapple!
She swims like custard!

He's as daft as custard!
Time is just like a cactus!
She swims like a pineapple!

# Visiting Grandad in the Home

His life is a half-circle
Of chairs by the TV.
His eyes come alive
And he waves at me,

But he calls me Simon,
And that's my dad's name,
And we talk about the weather
And the England game.

Then his face seems to slip,
His smile fades away
As he falls over backwards
Into yesterday.

And he talks to Grandma
Even though she isn't there,
And he's telling stories
To an empty chair.

And it's time for me to go
And he doesn't see me leave
And he won't know that I've been
But I really do believe

That the minutes I sit there
Mean an awful lot
Whether Grandad can remember them

Or not.

# Choir

OOOOOOOOOOO
OOOOOOOOOOO
OOOOOOOOOOO
OOOOOOOOOOO

## CHOIR IN WINTER

OOOOOCHOOOOOOO
OCHOOOCHOOOOOO
CHOOCHOOACHOOO
ACHOOCHOOACHOO

## CHOIR WITH SORE THROATS

OOOOOOOOOOOOOOOOOOOOO
OOOO OOOOO OOOOOOOOOO
O O  O  O    OOOOOOOOOO
OOOOOOOO

# CHOIR WITH TWO NEW MEMBERS

OOOOOOOOOOOOOOO
OOOOOOOAOOOOOO
OOOOOOOOOOOOEOO
OOOOOOOOOOOOOOO

# CHOIR ATTACKED BY WASPS

OOOZZOOZOOZOOZOZO
ZZOOZOZOZOZOZZZZOO
ZZZZOOOOZZZOOZZOZO

# Prove It

Teacher said, write a poem,
so I did. I wrote
'Happy Birthday to you
Happy Birthday to you
Happy Birthday dear me
Happy Birthday to you'

Teacher said, that's not a poem.
I said It is. It rhymes,
it's got rhythm.

Teacher said You didn't write that poem.
I said I did. Sixty-seven years ago,
in my house near the river.

Teacher said, you're only sixteen.
I said So What. I wrote it
before I was born. In my mam's belly
in her house near the river.

Teacher said, you didn't write that poem.
I said Prove it.

Outside our house the river flowed.
The river of poetry.
the river I wrote.

# Washing Line

Socks on the washing line
walk in sky,

Gloves on the washing line
wave goodbye!

Skirts on the washing line
dance in air,

with pants on the washing line
pair by pair!

Washing line stretched
from there to there

Yes, washing line stretched
from there to there!

# Bus Stop

When the bus comes round the corner
We all stand and shout

'Bus stop at the
Bus stop!

Stop bus,
Let people out!'

Because the bus stops at the
Bus stop

And lets us all
Get in!

# Odd Sock

He's been here. Here in the drawer,
here in the washbin.

Here in the washing machine.
Here on the washing line.

Oddsock. Remember his name.

He's out there somewhere
with a pile of socks.

He's planning World Domination.
He's planning The Sock Plague.

Oddsock. Remember his name.

You can't see him. Or hear him.
Stay up all night if you like.

He'll still get the sock.
The moment's it's off your foot.

Oddsock. Oddsock.

# This Poem Is Soooo *Prop*

Cool used to be
A really cool word,
Then it warmed up slightly
And flew away on old lady's wings.

Then Wicked
Was Wicked
Now it's more ancient than my Uncle Jack,
(That's my ancient Uncle Jack we're talking about.)

So now I invent a new word every day
Just to keep one step ahead.

Last week I was
Snail, Wallpaper, Buckle, Hen's teeth,
But they're so last week.

Yesterday I was Crocodile
But that's Yesterday's thing.

Today I'm *prop*,
The *proppest* kid on our street

Till tomorrow.

# So Cool

I'm so cool
It hurts. Ow.
That's me:
Cool as a knife.
A cool knife.
So cool
I'm frozen. Brrr.
That's me:
Hip as a snowman.
Er. That's
Not quite
What I meant. Ow.
So cool, Cool as

A trifle. No.
That's silly.
I'm cool. So Cool.
Cool as
A cool thing.
A really cool thing.
Er. I'm cool.
OK. Shut up.
I'm cool. I am.
Cool as a lollipop.
I'm not crying.
No. That's
Cool Sweat.
Shut up.
Just shut up.

# Flying into Mexico City

Below the dark sky the lights begin,
Then they multiply
To make a city of light.

This is a place where the air is thin,
Where a baby's cry
Hangs in the sweating night.

And the ground is getting closer
And the runway's getting nearer
And the feeling in my tightening chest
Is fear

And my arms are tired, so tired
From flapping
All the way across the sea.

# School Shirts

White, waving
From the midnight washing line

Or hanging limply
In the moonlight

Like ghosts.

The cat sits on the lawn,
Unafraid,
But what does the cat know?

# The Music I Like

The Music I like
Is very special music.

At this moment,
For instance,

I'm listening to the washing machine
Slowing down,

As the gerbil rattles
In its cage,

And my wife runs
Up the stairs

And my next door neighbour
Cuts his grass.

Music, very special music
Just listen . . .

# Turnip Head

Hollow out the turnip
Make the turnip head
Give him a smile
To wake the dead!

Give him a candle
Where his brain should be
Hang him from
The gallows tree . . .

Give him eyes
As dead as night
Flickering in
The candlelight

Hang him up
Till the candle dies
And smoke comes out
Of his turnip eyes

Then hear the children's
Awful screams
As the turnip man
Invades their dreams

As the turnip man
Invades their dreams . . .

# Night/Day

Night/Day
Night/Day
how / always been;
Night/Day
Night/Day
dark / light machine.
Night/Day
Night/Day
how / all start?
Night/Day
Night/Day
Universe / beating heart.
Night/Day
Night/Day
nothing / blinding flash?
Night/Day
Night/Day
or was it just a / ?

# Remote Control Patrol

Remote control
Remote control
I'm on remote control patrol!

Down the cushion
Behind the chair
I've been searching
Everywhere.

Under the magazines
In the shed
In the cupboard
With the crusty bread.

Remote control
Remote control
I'm on remote control patrol!

Where can it be?
Where can it be?
I don't know
So don't ask me!

Is it with the goldfish
In its bowl?
With the rabbit
In its hole?

In the ground
With a snuffling mole?
Or sitting on the ice
At the cold North Pole?

Remote control
Remote control
I'm on remote control patrol!

# Index of First Lines

# A selected list of poetry books available from Macmillan

The prices shown below are correct at the time of going to press. However, Macmillan Publishers reserve the right to show new retail prices on covers which may differ from those previously advertised.

| | |
|---|---|
| **The Evil Doctor Mucus Spleen**<br>Poems chosen by Paul Cookson | 0 330 39717 6<br>£3.99 |
| **The Very Best of Paul Cookson** | 0 330 48014 6<br>£3.99 |
| **Who Rules the School?**<br>Poems chosen by Paul Cookson | 0 330 35199 0<br>£3.50 |
| **Superheroes**<br>Fearless poems, chosen by Paul Cookson | 0 330 48262 9<br>£2.99 |
| **Tongue Twisters and Tonsil Twizzlers**<br>Poems chosen by Paul Cookson | 0 330 34941 4<br>£3.50 |
| **Let's Twist Again**<br>Poems chosen by Paul Cookson | 0 330 37559 8<br>£3.50 |
| **Ridiculous Relatives**<br>Poems chosen by Paul Cookson | 0 330 37105 3<br>£3.50 |

All Macmillan titles can be ordered at your local bookshop or are available by post from:

**Book Service by Post**
**PO Box 29, Douglas, Isle of Man IM99 1BQ**

Credit cards accepted. For details:
Telephone: 01624 675137
Fax: 01624 670923
E-mail: bookshop@enterprise.net

**Free postage and packing in the UK.**
Overseas customers: add £1 per book (paperback)
and £3 per book (hardback).